THIS BOOK BELONGS TO

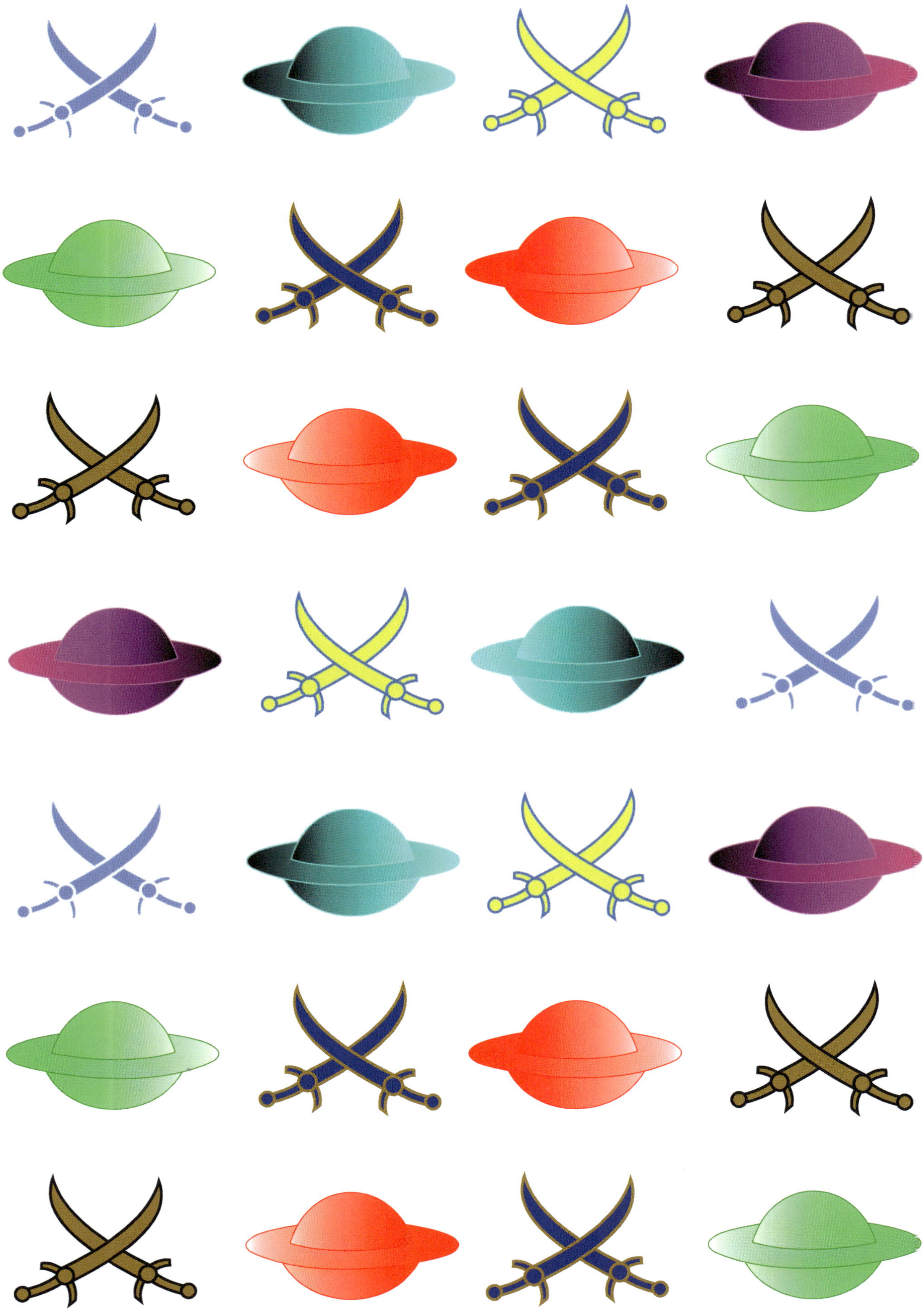

First published in 2023 By D. J. Barrass Publishing

ISBN 978-1-3999-6480-7

THE SHIP SWAP

Daniel & Jonathan Barrass

One fine day, in the middle of the sea,
Rugged pirates were roaming free
Until the captain spotted something strange in the sky —
It was shiny, round, and way up high.

“Look at that!” said the captain aloud.
The pirates looked, yet saw nothing but a cloud.

In a flash, the object was hovering over the sea.

“Oh no!” said the captain. “What on earth can it be?”

All of a sudden, a door opened wide,
And there was an alien looking down from inside.
"Wow!" said the alien. "I like your ship.
Please, may I take it for a trip?"

The captain was oh so stunned,
But saw a chance to have some fun.
"I have an idea — we can swap for a while."
"That's great!" said the alien, with a big smile.

The alien jumped onto the deck,
And the pirates were teleported — now that's high-tech!

“How do I work this craft?” the captain grumbled.
As he said that, the engines rumbled!

They were in space within the blink of an eye.
"I'm scared!" said a pirate, and he started to cry.

Huge asteroids raged deep in space —
It really was a dangerous place!

The spaceship was on course for the alien's planet. It can't be as bad as the journey, can it?

The captain was worried,
as it was a mysterious land —

It had orange trees,
and bright purple sand.

Meanwhile, at sea, big waves rose high!
“I don’t like this — I'm only used to the sky!”
The alien was scared, as it was getting dark.
And what’s that in the water? It looks like a shark!

The alien started to think about home.
He didn't like this planet — he was all alone!

"I miss the pink sky and the shiny green rocks —
I miss my pet cat with his bright blue socks."

The pirates began to walk around,
But their feet were sinking into the ground.
The sand was gobbling up the crew.
"Oh no!" said the captain. "What shall we do?"

From the orange trees, an alien appeared.
He had dazzling green skin and a fluffy blue beard.

The pirates began to scream and shout.
“Please help get us out!”

The alien nodded his head and waved his hand,
And just like that, the pirates were out of the sand.

“We want to go home to where things make sense
And everything feels far less tense.
We miss the waves and the ocean so blue —
Even the sharks, we miss them too.”

“Don’t worry,” said the alien. “I’ll take you home —
Just climb inside this shiny dome.”

The sea calmed and the sun came out,
But would the alien ever get home? He was beginning to doubt
Until he spotted something in the sky —
It was shiny, round, and way up high.
"Hooray, hooray, my friends are here.
I'm going home — no need to fear!"

The pirates were back where they belonged.
They were so happy, they broke into song.

The aliens both waved goodbye,

And in a flash, they shot off into the sky.

THE END

Printed in Great Britain
by Amazon

31326422R00018